THE
GASTANK
OF MY
HEART

THE
GASTANK
OF MY
HEART

RICHARD
THOMPSON

The Caitlin Press

The Caitlin Press
P.O. Box 2387, Station B
Prince George, B.C. V2N 2S6
Canada

Cover design by Gaye Hammond
The financial assistance of the British Columbia
Cultural Fund is gratefully acknowledged. The
expertise and advice of Harbour Publishing has
been invaluable.
Printed and bound in Canada

Canadian Cataloguing in Publication Data

Thompson, Richard, 1951–
    Gastank of my heart

    ISBN 0-920576-38-9

    I. Title.
PS8589.H53G3 1991   C813'.54   C91-091832-5
PR9199.3.T496G3 1991*

The Gastank of My Heart
is dedicated to my family

CONTENTS

WHEN TV COMES TO THE VAST NORTHERN PRAIRIE

When TV first comes to the Vast Northern Prairie, it doesn't come in all at once. It creeps up—grey ghosts of Ed Sullivan and Dennis the Menace drifting like ice fog from willow clump to willow clump over the frozen stubble fields.

"THEY GOT *LEAVE IT TO BEAVER* OUT IN ROLLA!" shouts my dad. He always shouts for three or four hours after he gets off the D9— till the noise gets out of his head.

"I'M GOING TO MOVE THE ANTENNA AROUND. YOU TELL ME IF ANYTHING COMES IN!" He climbs up onto the roof and starts fiddling with the antenna while the rest of us clack the channel knob around and around and watch for signs of life. Sometimes we get a bit of sound with no picture and sometimes we get a picture with no sound and once for a couple seconds we get a picture and sound at the same time – about two beeps of a Road Runner cartoon.

Well, it does come eventually – only one channel and no colour, of course. That first Saturday, Gramma walks over from her house to watch our TV. She brings her crochet hook and a ball of white twine and a doily that's about half finished. She sits down on the couch and starts working her fingers back and forth, back and forth, using that hook to tie tiny, intricate knots in the twine.

"TIME FOR CHAMPIONSHIP RASSLING LIVE FROM MAPLE LEAF GARDENS IN TORONTO," shouts my dad, coming in the door and flinging his jacket over the back of a kitchen chair. He turns on the TV, sits down in his Lazy-Boy chair and tips back like he's been watching Championship Rassling Live From Toronto all his life.

Gramma doesn't seem to be paying much attention at first. But about the time Haystack Calhoun climbs up onto the top rope intending to jump off and squash Johnny Otis, her fingers start working faster. Midway into the tag team match between Lou Tamino and Bruno Getz on one side and the Hillbilly Cousins on the other side – when BOTH the Hillbilly Cousins jump into the ring and start rassling Lou Tamino, and you can see that Bruno Getz really wants to get in there and even things up, but it's against the rules, so he won't do it – that's when Gramma throws down her crocheting and starts yelling,

"THEY CAN'T DO THAT! WHERE'S THE REF-
EREE! GET THAT GUY OUT OF THERE!"
Then it's the last bout of a best two out of
three falls, no time limit match. Sven the Swe-
dish Meatball has been giving Wee Willy Wat-
son a really bad time. Wee Willy has been kicked
in the head so many times he's just wandering
around the ring like a stupid person. But, finally,
Meatball does one mean thing too many, and
Wee Willy gets mad. Meatball slingshots Willy
into the ropes, but when Willy comes off he
comes off feet first and drop kicks Meatball in
the side of the head. They both hit the mat . . . I
don't know what happens after that, because
Gramma catches me around the head and locks
me in tight against her big, soft bosom. I can't see,
and I can hardly breath. I kick and try to call out,
"LET ME GO, GRAMMA! I CAN'T BREATHE!"
But she just locks on tighter and starts twisting, and
all I can say is "MMMMMPHHH! HUHNNN!"
Maybe Haystack Calhoun could get out of that
headlock, but I'm stuck, so I just lie really still
and try to save my air so I won't die. Eventually
Leave It To Beaver comes on, and Gramma loos-
ens off her grip. I squirm free and run outside
and gulp down big lungfuls of cold, sparkly win-
ter air.

One Saturday afternoon, a couple months later,
we're watching TV the same as usual. About half-
way into the program, Haystack Calhoun does
something. My dad and I have never been able

to agree on just what it was. My dad says Haystack bit Johnny Otis' ear, but I think he hit the referee. My mom says she doesn't know and doesn't care. Gramma won't talk about it. But whatever it was gets Gramma mad – I mean really mad.

All of a sudden, she jumps up off the couch and squinches at the screen in an ugly way and starts hollering, "That's going TOO far, MISTER Calhoun! THAT'S GOING TOO FAR!!!"

Then she stomps out of the room, stomps through the kitchen and stomps out the back door and into the snow.

"WHAT'S WRONG WITH MA?" my dad shouts. "She's mad at Haystack Calhoun," I say.

"What's wrong with Mom?" asks my mom, coming into the livingroom, wiping her hands on her apron.

"She's mad at Haystack Calhoun," I say.

"WANT ME TO GO AFTER HER?" shouts my dad.

"She'll be alright," says my mom.

"She's just mad at Haystack Calhoun is all," I say, but nobody is listening.

Gramma doesn't come over the next week.

"Do you suppose she's still mad at us?" asks my mom.

"It's Haystack Calhoun she's mad at," I say.

"WELL, IF SHE DON'T GET OVER HER MAD REAL SOON SHE'S GOING TO MISS THE RASSLING," shouts my dad. He switches on the TV and settles back in his Lazy-Boy recliner rocker.

Right after the second match, Fred Bambini is interviewing Haystack Calhoun. That's when it happens. Off camera there's a lot of caffuffle and Fred says, "What in heaven's name!" and Haystack starts to say something, and his mouth drops open. This big black shape comes hurtling out of the audience and hits old Haystack right in the middle of his interview. He and the black shape and Fred Bambini all go down. The camera woggles around and up and down for a minute and then focuses for a second. You can see Haystack running toward the dressing room with this woman running after him shaking her fist. Then the sign NETWORK TROUBLE TEMPORARY comes on the screen, and that Network Trouble Temporary music.

"That was Gramma!" I yell.

"WHAT?"

"That was Gramma chasing Haystack Calhoun!" I yell. I'm jumping up and down on the couch, I'm so excited.

"Stop yelling!" says my mom.

"It was! Didn't you see her?"

"THAT'S RIDICULOUS," yells my dad.

"If you two don't stop yelling, I'm going to shut that thing off!"

"It was Gramma," I say, but under my breath, because I don't want my mom to shut the TV off.

The next week Gramma is back again, and she brings her crochet hook and her twine.

"WHERE DID YOU GET TO LAST WEEK, MA?" my dad shouts.

Gramma doesn't answer, just keeps on working her fingers back and forth. I move over onto the couch, and I whisper to her, "I know where you were, Gramma. I saw you on the TV."

"That's silly," she says, but her eyes twinkle when she says it.

"DID YOU SEE THAT, MA!" my dad shouts. "OLD HAYSTACK JUST PUT OTIS THROUGH THE THRESHING MACHINE!"

Gramma doesn't say anything, just keeps working her fingers back and forth.

"OTIS ISN'T GOING TO COME BACK FROM THIS ONE, MA! HAYSTACK HAS HIM IN THE MANURE SPREADER!"

Gramma doesn't answer, but she pulls me over closer to her. I'm afraid she's going to get me in another headlock, but she winks at me and says really quietly, "It isn't real, you know. Me and Haystack and Johnny Otis went out for Chinese food in Toronto together, and they told me all about it."

"Really?"

Gramma grins and nods.

I was right!

"Dad," I cry, jumping up.

"WHAT IS IT, SON?" my dad shouts.

"Gramma..." I glance over at Gramma. She shakes her head just a little bit, and I know she wants it to be our secret about how she went out for Chinese food with Haystack Calhoun and Johnny Otis, so I say, "Gramma wasn't mad at us. She was just mad at Haystack. Just like I said. Isn't that right, Gramma?"

"That's right," says Gramma, "but I'm over my mad now."

THE WORRIES

Sure, people had Worries before that, and they still do. In fact, Dora Ritter keeps a whole house full of them, and she'd be really lonely if anybody came and took them away. But, as anybody who lived in New Totem that spring will tell you—there are worries and there are Worries. The Worries that fell upon the town in the April of that year were definitely of the latter variety.

Ma Trotter was up early that morning, putting a pot of fudge on to cook for breakfast. It was still dark out—only the stars shining. Ma saw them coming.

"There were so many of them that the street looked like a river of grey slime flowing along!" she said later.

By the time the people woke up and got moving for the day it was too late. Everybody in that town was worried like they never were worried before. And it's funny, those Worries seemed to be able to find just the right person to latch onto.

The Trotter baby had three or four New Teeth Coming In Worries sitting in his crib with him, making him fuss and cry all day and all night.

There was a Big Dogs Biting You Worry sitting on the Spencer's doorstep, and little Meghan wouldn't go out to play.

Dougie Bower had a Bullies In the Bush Worry riding in his lunch kit when he headed off for school.

And Olive Rigley had Can't Do Nothing With It Worries all tangled up in her long hair.

Arnie Dewhurst, the catskinner, had Break Down and Go Broke Worries climbing all over his D9 Caterpillar Crawler Tractor.

Arnie's little daughter, Brandy, waving bye to Arnie in the morning, had Fatherless Child Worries whispering to her about how her daddy was sure to drive his cat into a muskeg bog and disappear forever.

Gladys Friend had a horrible Getting Fat Worry. One minute it would be telling her, "Hey Blimpo, when you going to do something about the spare tire." The next minute it would be in the kitchen baking an angel food cake.

Stan Walsh at Walsh's Home Furnishings had so many Worries clutching at his ankles that he could barely shuffle down the street to the store, and the Mayor had so many Worries hanging off his hands he was all scrouched over like a gorilla when he walked.

Some people had so many Worries sitting on them that they couldn't even get up, just sat in the same chair from morning till night and then rolled into bed and lay awake all night with those Worries tickling them and jabbing them in the ribs.

The only person in town who was happy was Dora Ritter. Since her kids grew up, Dora had been lonely in that big house of hers down by the Civic Arena. So when a gaggle of Worries came knocking at her door that morning, Dora put the coffee pot on.

Everybody else grumbled and moaned about their Worries, but Dora loved hers. She crocheted them lace collars and booties and kept them in a neat row along the back of her couch. When neighbours would come over for coffee, she'd show them off as proud as a porcupine.

The Worries hung around all springtime.

"It's going to be a worrisome summer," moaned Gladys Friend as she tried to brush off a Worry that was telling her how terrible she looked in her new pink sundress.

"I can't go out and play, Mom!" whined Dougie Bower. "Jimmy Jackson said he's going to beat me up!"

The Mayor's knuckles got dustier and dustier.

Everybody but Dora Ritter was moaning about something.

But then about the middle of June the word started to get around, posters started appearing on the telephone poles. The Worried Man was coming to town! You must have heard about him; he had a lot of big hit songs on the radio. I don't remember his real name—just remember he was called the Worried Man—but I know he was pretty famous for a while there. Olive Rigley went down to the Civic Arena at dawn on the day of the show to be sure she got a ticket. By six o'clock in the evening most of the town was lined up behind her. But when the ticket booth opened the man shook his head and said sorry, they were all sold out.

"What do you mean!" yelled Olive. "I was the very first in line!"

"Well, I don't know about that," said the man, "but the place is full. Look for yourself."

Olive peeked in the door. The bleachers were packed! Her very own Can't Do Nothing With It Worry was sitting right down in front next to Arnie Dewhurst's Break Down and Go Broke Worry. The place was packed with Worries.

"The tickets are all gone!" Olive wailed loud enough so everyone could hear right down to the back of the line. "We aren't going to get to see the Worried Man!"

But people didn't seem to be too worried—for a change. Most headed off home to watch *My Three Sons* on TV. Olive and a few others hung around and peeked in at the door. The Worried Man moaned and whined his way through all his big hits: Pieces of My Heart, Momma Don't Love Me, and Olive's favourite: Standing Here Naked Looking Like a Fool. The Worries stomped and hollered. Then he sang a new song that hadn't even been on the radio yet—Worry That Worry Till the Juice Runs Down! The Worries were up dancing by the time he finished. He sang for a couple of hours, every song sad enough to break your heart and stomp on the pieces. Olive Rigley was bawling her eyes out, but the Worries were laughing and hanging from the rafters.

Finally, the Worried Man stood up and said, "That's all, folks! Been real nice singing for you!" He walked out back of the Arena and opened the door of his big blue bus. Well, all of a sudden, like a river of grey slime, those Worries came pouring out the back door of the Arena. They swept the Worried Man up and onto the bus and kept on packing in after him.

Olive watched with her eyes popping and her mouth hanging open. "Look at them all!" she said. "They can't all fit in there! No way!"

But they did. In a couple of minutes, the Civic Arena was empty as an echo. When the door of the big blue bus sooshed closed there wasn't a Worry in sight, except for Dora Ritter's sitting in a tidy row on her front porch drinking cream soda and eating hickory-flavoured shoe-string potato chips.

The Worried Man drove away, and he took all those Worries with him.

"What's he do with all them Worries?" Honey Dewhurst was wondering about that as she was making Arnie's lunch the next morning, so she asked Arnie. Arnie sucked the fat off a piece of bacon rind and laid it down on the edge of his plate. He sopped up some yolk on a bit of toast and popped it in his mouth. He was thinking.

"I suppose he takes them down to Edmonton," he said at last. "Seems like they can never get enough Worries in the big city . . ."

"That doesn't seem fair," said Honey. "Do you think that's fair, Arnie?"

"Honey," said Arnie. He swallowed the last of his tea and started to put on his coat. "I don't know if it's fair or not, but I'll tell you—I'm sure not going to worry about it."

SEVENTY-SIX
BLANKETS

On the afternoon of the day that Yvonne MacDonald told her best friend, Annette Muskie, about her engagement to Ivor Dressler, an arctic air mass swept down across the Vast Northern Prairie.

Even as they talked, the town of New Totem was beginning to seize up solid. "I know he lives a ways out of town and we won't get to visit much, Annette. But he's such a good dancer!"

By four o'clock nothing moved. The tires on all the cars and trucks froze to the ground so nobody could drive anywhere even if they could get their engines started.

"I know he doesn't make much money. Trapping isn't high paying work these days. But, Annette, what a dancer!"

The telephone lines were plugged with words that had congealed halfway to where they were going. "I know I'm a city girl, Annette, but I don't need a fancy house. And I don't need to be going to Bingo every Tuesday at the Immaculata Hall."

Tuesday Night Bingo was cancelled that week anyway.

"All I need is my Ivor and a few square feet of floor for dancing!"

But somehow or other, by the end of that week, everybody in New Totem who needed to know, and a lot who didn't, knew about Yvonne's upcoming wedding to Ivor Dressler.

And every one of those people, sitting listening to the radio talking about how the wind-chill factor outside was minus ninety-eight degrees, they conjured up a picture of Yvonne sitting in that cabin up on Lynx Creek shivering and crying as the fire in the oil drum stove froze into a mass of orange and yellow icicles. Every one of those people shivered in sympathy, and every one of them had the same wonderful idea.

Yvonne MacDonald of New Totem was wed to Ivor Dressler of up on Lynx Creek in the Wolfendale Hall in New Totem on February 2. There was a dance at the Legion that evening and all the girls in New Totem found out how Ivor could dance.

The next afternoon guests were invited over to Yvonne's parents' house to watch her open the gifts.

The first package Yvonne opened was a comforter from her best friend, Annette, that Annette had sewn herself with a little help from her sister-in-law Arlette. "I didn't want you to be cold out there in the bush," Annette said, and Yvonne laughed.

The second present, from Shelley and Grant Freemantle, was a white wool blanket from the Hudson's Bay Store with a red stripe and a blue stripe on each end. "We didn't want you to freeze up there before we have a chance to come and visit," said Shelley, and Yvonne laughed.

The third present, from Yvonne's aunt Dolores, was a crocheted bedspread. "I was going to make you a runner for the back of the couch like I made for Tammy when she got married," said Dolores, "but I thought about it and decided that something more practical would be better. I hope you like it." Yvonne smiled.

By the end of the afternoon, Yvonne's pile of gifts included four handmade comforters, seven white blankets with stripes from the Hudson's Bay Store, six pairs of sleeping bags (the kind that zip together), twenty-one blankets from the Eaton's catalogue, three Miracle Space Age Blankets from the K-tel advertisements on TV, five quilts stuffed with genuine goose down, two buffalo robes, three sets of matching men's and ladies' red flannel long underwear and one crocheted bedspread.

The guests were pretty quiet as Yvonne opened that last package and held up the seventh white blanket with stripes from the Hudson's Bay Store, but Yvonne smiled.

"Not much dancing room in here, Vonnie," said Ivor, as he and his bride crossed over the threshold of the little cabin on Lynx Creek.

"That's okay," said Yvonne.

"Our wedding presents take up quite a bit of room." Blankets and comforters were stacked up all along the south wall, right to the ceiling. "Come spring, we can add on a new room for the blankets."

Toward the end of February, another arctic air mass rolled out of the north and settled like a dead dog's ghost into the hollows along Lynx Creek. Ivor stuffed another couple logs in the oil drum heater, and Yvonne pulled on another pair of wool socks. But about bedtime, there was a knock at the door. Ivor pulled on his parka and opened the door.

"Eric!" he cried. "What are you doing here! Come in!" He stood aside to let Eric into the room, but Eric stood there, didn't say anything, didn't move.

"Vonnie!" called Ivor. "It's Eric Coulson from up the creek. He's froze solid. Help me bring him in." Yvonne put on her parka and helped her husband wrestle their rigid neighbour through the door. They were as careful as they could be, but his left hand brushed against the sill, and the baby finger broke off and fell to the floor with a tinkling like broken crystal.

"Careful!" said Ivor.

They propped him up by the oil drum heater. "He looks awful," said Yvonne. He did too. His face and hands were blue-white and almost transparent, like Coke bottle glass. In fact, he was so stiff and still he might have actually been made out of Coke bottle glass.

"Might as well play a few hands of crib while we wait for him to thaw," said Ivor, and he got down the cards and the crib board made from a deer's horn. "Don't you think we should do something?" asked Yvonne.

"Nothing we can do," said Ivor, "except wait. Your crib." The newlyweds played cribbage until dawn. Every couple hands, Ivor got up and turned Eric a quarter of a turn.

As the sun came up and poked weakly through the curtains, Yvonne stood and declared, "This is no good, Ivor! He's as stiff now as he was when we brought him in. His clothes are so hot they're starting to smoke, and he's still stiff as a board."

"The fire box is full," said Ivor, "The damper's full open. What else can we do?"

"Fetch in the boiler," said Yvonne.

"It's too cold to be thinking about taking a bath, Vonnie," said Ivor, as Yvonne lifted the tin wash boiler onto the heater and began filling it with bucketfuls of snow from outside the door.

"It's not for me, silly," she said, "It's for Eric." When the water was hot, they lifted the boiler onto the floor, and stood the frozen man in it clothes and all.

Yvonne picked up the cards. "Let's play for a penny a point," she said. The girl from New Totem and her new husband played cribbage till the sun went down. Every three or four hands they would have to lift Eric out of the water and put it back on the heater to warm up again.

Around supper time, Ivor got up and poked at Eric a bit. "Is he any softer?" asked Yvonne.

"Still solid as ever," said Ivor, "maybe we should just hang him in a tree till spring."

"Let's try one more thing," said Yvonne. "Help me put him into bed." Reluctantly, he helped her lift the frozen man onto the bed.

"Okay, let's get him covered up." Yvonne started piling on wedding presents. In a few minutes Eric Coulson was buried under four handmade comforters, seven white blankets with stripes from the Hudson's Bay Store, six pairs of sleeping bags (the kind that zip together), twenty-one blankets from the Eaton's catalogue, three Miracle Space Age Blankets from the K-tel advertisements on TV, five quilts stuffed with genuine goose down, and two buffalo robes.

"Good!" said Yvonne, as she threw on Aunt Dolores' crocheted bedspread. "Whose deal is it?" That trapper and his young bride played cribbage all that night.

"Fifteen-two, fifteen-four, fifteen-six and a pair is eight," said Yvonne, blinking in the feeble light of dawn. "I win again."

"Nope!" said Ivor. "It's your crib, so I count first. Fifteen-two, fifteen-four, fifteen-six, and six are twelve. I win."

"That was your crib!" declared Yvonne, "I threw you the two and the Jack."

"No! It was your crib."

"No! It was your crib!" yelled Yvonne, "Ivor Dressler, if I knew you were a cheater, I would never have married you!"

"He's right, Yvonne! It was your crib."

"You keep out of this, Eric!" yelled Yvonne. And then she realized what she'd said. "Eric, you're thawed!"

After a breakfast consisting of four bowls of Sunny Boy Porridge, half a dozen eggs, most of a side of bacon, hash browns and toast, Eric was feeling warm enough to crawl out from under the blankets and sit by the oil drum heater.

"I don't know how to thank you two," he said.

"No need! No need!" protested Ivor.

"But I was wondering," Eric continued, "if I could ask you one more favour."

"Anything at all!" declared Yvonne.

"I still feel a bit chilled. I think I'll go back home and curl up with a book for a while. Would you mind lending me a couple of those blankets?"

"Take them all!" said Yvonne and Ivor together.

So they lent their neighbour a toboggan and he loaded up the four handmade comforters, seven white blankets with stripes from the Hudson's Bay Store, six pairs of sleeping bags (the kind that zip together), twenty-one blankets from the Eaton's catalogue, three Miracle Space Age Blankets from the K-tel advertisements on TV, five quilts stuffed with genuine goose down, and two buffalo robes.

"You best keep this," said Eric, handing back the crocheted bedspread, "it's too fancy for my place!"

Yvonne and Ivor waved until he was out of sight and then went back inside the cabin. "The cabin looks positively palatial with that stack of blankets gone," said Yvonne.

"It does," said Ivor. "Would you care to dance, my princess?"

"Charmed," said Yvonne.

Eric Coulson went to sleep under that pile of blankets, and slept till the end of April. Then he got up, shaved, and walked down the creek, never to return. Several families of squirrels made their homes amongst the blankets, comforters, and sleeping bags that he left behind.

Yvonne never told Annette what had become of the hand-sewn comforter, and Annette never asked.

Ivor and Yvonne never missed the blankets. Whenever it got so cold that the fire froze in the stove, they just put on their three pairs of matching men's and lady's red flannel long underwear and danced together by the light of the coal oil lamp until the weather broke.

OLÉ!

Ma Trotter, the Fudge Lady, had two daughters. Honey was the elder, and Lynnette was, by default, the younger. Like their mother, both girls became, in those days of white margarine and running boards on pick-up trucks, culinary legends throughout the width and breadth of the Vast Northern Prairie.

I could go on at some length about Honey's butter tarts and Honey's barbecued ribs and Honey's cabbage rolls and Honey's matrimonial squares and Honey's corned beef hash But I'm not going to. I'm going to tell you, instead, about Lynnette's famous chili. Olé!

Lynnette was working as a cook for the Bolger Bros. Construction Company in a small bush camp about a hundred and fifty miles north of New Totem. She had been on the job for about three weeks when Orville Potts, the foreman, came into the cook shack one afternoon and handed her a fat, greasy book.

"This here is the United Farm Wives of Alberta Cookbook, Lynnette," he said. "I borrowed it from my wife, Corinne. I'd like you to take a look through this book and see if you can't find something to make for supper."

Lynnette had been making grilled cheese sandwiches and tinned cream of tomato soup for every lunch and supper since she'd started. She made toast for breakfast.

"Sure, Orville," she said.

That night she served her famous chili.

The men dished great heaping mounds of the stuff onto their plates and dug in with gusto. Two or three spoonfuls in, Orville stopped digging. He looked to the left. Harve Westaway, the grader operator, had stopped digging and was sitting there with his jaw clapped tight shut and his ears turning flaming red. Orville looked to the right. Wayne Clarkson, one of the cat-skinners, was sitting there with his cheeks squirrel-big with gobs of chili. He was really still, not moving a muscle, and tears were running down his cheeks.

Orville grimaced and swallowed. You could hear the chili hit his stomach. It made a dull thud like a boot dropping on a bunkhouse floor. Each of the others swallowed: THUD! THUD! THUD! THUD! THUD! THUD!

"Pass me down the bread and butter," said Orville.

Lynnette's feelings were hurt, of course.

"I followed the stupid recipe!" she muttered, as she flung the rest of the chili, pot and all, out into the bush behind the cook shack.

"Well, if they don't like my chili, they can eat grilled cheese sandwiches till Doomsday!"

And so saying, she flung Corinne Potts' United Farm Wives of Alberta Cookbook into the bush, too. Both the pot and the book landed on the edge of a muskeg bog.

Now, every catskinner, and every friend of a catskinner on the Vast Northern Prairie can tell you a tale or two meant to illustrate to the uninitiated that you cannot drive a D9 Cat across a muskeg bog.

But, for some reason, that is exactly what Wayne Clarkson attempted to do the very next morning. After breakfast, he climbed on his D9 and walked it straight into the muskeg bog out behind the cook shack! The bog slurped him down like a raw oyster, smacked its lips and sighed contentedly.

"Holy Romoli! Wayne's gone!" moaned Orville Potts. "What are we going to tell his mother?"

"What was he doing, driving out into a muskeg bog? He knows better than that!"

"That chili of Lynnette's must have killed off a few of his brain cells."

"Half asleep, more than likely. I know, I didn't sleep worth beans myself – excuse the pun. Kept burping all night."

Lynnette started to wail. "Hey you guys! It's not my fault if Wayne Clarkson doesn't know how to drive a Cat. Don't blame me!"

At that moment, the ground began to tremble. The surface of the bog started to swell. With a great woosh, the bog exploded, sending mud and grass, twisty roots and small animals, dead snags and bits of bush straight up into the air.

"Look out!" yelled Orville Potts. Mud and grass, twisty roots and small animals, dead snags and bits of bush, came raining down all around them. Then, with an earsplitting crash, a D9 Cat smashed out of the sky and right through the cook shack roof. The last things to land were a stainless steel cooking pot and a United Farm Wives of Alberta Cookbook.

"Where's Wayne?" someone hollered.

Wayne was still riding on the Cat, and he put her in gear and drove out through the north wall of the cook shack.

Frank and Percy Bolger flew up to the camp that afternoon and, of course, they wanted to know how their cook shack came to be all smashed up.

"Near as I can figure," Orville Potts told them, "when the bog swallowed up Wayne and the Cat, it swallowed up that pot of Lynnette's chili too. And as I can testify, as soon as you got some of that chili in you, you get an overpowering urge to belch."

The ground began to shake.

"Look out! She's fixing to let loose with another!"

And sure enough, there was a horrendous roar and a couple of seconds later, mud and grass, twisty roots and small animals, dead snags and bits of bush came raining down all around them.

"I heard that there's been roots and chipmunks and things falling on the main street in New Totem a hundred and fifty miles south," said Percy. "How long is this going to go on?"

"I don't know," said Orville. "That was a big pot of chili."

No one knows for sure how long the bog might have gone on belching mud and grass, twisty roots and small animals, dead snags and bits of bush into the air. But after two weeks, it was still belching, and people were getting upset. The mayor of New Totem went to see the Bolger Bros. A bunch of farmers from up around Clayhurst came to complain how their chickens were getting owly. The Catholic Women's League came brandishing a good sized rock that had fallen in the middle of Gay Spencer's Lemon Chiffon Cake at their Harvest Tea and Bazaar. Frank and Percy decided that something had to be done.

The next day a Northern Prairie Air DC 3 swept in over the bog and, between belches, dumped in four forty-five gallon drums full of Eno Fruit Salts.

The bog belched one last tremendous belch and was silent.

Lynnette is waiting on tables in the Gateway Cafe now. There's chili on the menu. The chef at the Gateway makes a decent chili. But nobody orders it when Lynnette's working.

One guy did, and when Lynnette brought it to the table, he said, "You didn't cook this, did you Lynnette?"

He was joking.

Lynnette smiled sweetly and tipped the whole bowl onto his head.

Olé.

TUB-O-LARD

One afternoon, Ma Trotter was heading home through the willow flats carrying Little Andrew. She came round the first bend in the path, and there blocking the path was a great greasy giant of a man—half again as tall as a regular man and three times as wide!

"Hi there, Ma," the big man said. "So that's the new baby I heard about," he said, "I heard he was sweet enough to eat, and it seems I heard right."

He licked his fat lips and some spit dribbled down his chin.

Ma smiled a sort of a kind of smile and said, "Well, thank you, for saying so."

"People call me Tub-o-Lard," the big man said. "I'm a hungry man," he said, "I guess that's why people call me that."

"It's been really nice to meet you, Tub-o-Lard," said Ma, "but we really should be getting home. Little Andrew needs his nap, you know."

Tub-o-Lard just stood there in the path. He didn't say, "See you later." He didn't wave good-bye. He said, "I'm hungry right now." And he shot his eyes at Little Andrew and licked his fat lips.

Ma was worried. She had two other children at home, two grown-up girls, Honey and Lynnette. But she still didn't want that greasy giant eating up her baby.

"Speaking of hungry," she said really quick, "I've got a big pot of cabbage rolls in the oven right this minute. Why don't you come and have a plate or two of cabbage rolls with us, Tub-o-Lard."

"Nah!" said Tub-o-Lard, "I've been eating too many cabbage rolls." He looked at the baby and sucked on his big black teeth.

"If you don't feel like cabbage rolls, I could make you up some corned beef hash," said Ma.

"Nah!" said Tub-o-Lard. "I've been eating too much corned beef hash." He bent down and chucked Little Andrew under the chin.

"I could make you some Spanish Rice," said Ma, "with big chunks of pork sausage mixed in it. Would you like that, Tub-o-Lard?"

"Nah!" said Tub-o-Lard. "I've been eating too much Spanish Rice." He grinned a black-toothed grin at the baby. "I was really thinking of some-thing – sweet . . ."

"You want something sweet!" said Ma. "Why didn't you say so? I'll make you a whole pot of fudge, just for yourself." When Ma said that, Tub-o-Lard started to smack his big lips together and his guts started making a noise like a bear rummaging in a garbage can.

"I heard about your fudge, Ma," he said. Everybody all across the Vast Northern Prairie had heard about Ma Trotter's famous chocolate fudge.

"Yeah, that sounds good."

Back at the house, Ma got down a big stainless steel pot. She put in all the stuff for fudge and mixed it together. She put it on the stove to cook. The fudge bubbled for as long as fudge has to bubble.

"I have to whip it around for a while," said Ma, lifting the big pot off the stove. "That's the real secret of great fudge—the whipping around."

So she whipped the hot fudge for as long as fudge has to be whipped. And then she poured it into pans to cool. But Tub-o-Lard couldn't wait for it to cool. He grabbed a spoon and slurped down the hot fudge like it was pudding—six big pans of it.

"That was good," he said, smacking his lips and rubbing his belly. "I think I'll go home and have a nap now, Ma."

He heaved himself out of his chair and left the house.

Some time later, Honey and Lynnette were watching Little Andrew while Ma was over playing canasta with old Mrs. Beamish. There was a knock at the door. Honey went to the door, carrying Little Andrew on her hip. She opened the door, and there was Tub-o-Lard standing on the porch.

"Hi there, Honey," he said. "How are you? And how's that sweet brother of yours?"

"We're fine," said Honey.

"Aren't you going to ask me how I'm doing?" asked Tub-o-Lard.

"How are you, Tub-o-Lard?" said Honey.

Tub-o-Lard grinned his black-toothed grin. "I'm hungry," he said.

"Maybe you should go down to the IGA and buy some food," said Honey. She tried to close the door, but Tub-o-Lard's big foot was blocking it open.

"I'm too hungry to walk that far," said Tub-o-Lard.

"We got some fudge that Ma made yesterday," said Honey.

"Nah!" said Tub-o-Lard. "I ate too much fudge last time I was here." He reached out a big hand and tussled Andrew's blonde curls. "Sweet baby," he said.

"I could fry you some pork chops and potatoes."

"Nah! I've been eating too much pork chops and potatoes." He pinched one of Little Andrew's fat cheeks.

"Would you like some shepherd's pie? It's fresh hot."

"Nah! I've been eating too much shepherd's pie. You know, that baby's skin looks a bit dry.

Did you ever think about dunking him in olive oil? Maybe just a pinch of oregano?"

"I know!" said Honey. "I'll make you up a batch of butter tarts!" When he heard that, Tub-o-Lard started smacking his big lips together and his guts started making a noise like a pickup truck with the muffler knocked off.

"I've heard about your butter tarts!" said Tub-o-Lard. Honey's butter tarts were almost as famous as her mother's fudge. "That sounds good."

"Okay," said Honey, "But you've got to wait on the porch, because Ma isn't home." So Tub-o-Lard sat down to wait. Honey handed the baby to Lynnette, and she set to work. She mixed the pastry, rolled it out, cut it in circles and lined muffin tins with the circles. Then she set to making the filling. She put in whatever it was that made her tarts so sweet and spicy, and she cooked it as long as it needed to be cooked. She filled up the pastry with the filling and baked those tarts for as long a tarts are supposed to bake.

"The tarts are cooked, Tub-o-Lard," she called. "They just got to cool down for a few minutes."

"Don't worry about that," called Tub-o-Lard. "Just bring them on out here!" So Honey brought out pan after pan of blistering hot butter tarts, and Tub-o-Lard chucked them down his throat, one hand and the other hand, until he'd eaten all sixteen dozen.

"That was good, Honey," he said. "Now I think I will go home and have a nap."

And he heaved himself up off the porch and walked away from there.

Some time later Lynnette was home alone with Little Andrew. They were playing in the back yard. It was a hot day. There were no trees in the backyard, no shade. "I'll be right back, Andrew," said Lynnette, and she went into to the house to get the baby a hat to cover his head.

When she came back, there was Tub-o-Lard bending over the boy, fixing to grab him up in his great huge hands. He was grinning his black-tooth grin and spit was dribbling down his chin.

"Tub-o-Lard!" yelled Lynnette.

Tub-o-Lard unbent really slowly and looked at Lynnette. "Hi, Lynnette," he said. "I was just saying 'coochy goo' to your little brother. I swear, Lynnette, the only thing sweeter than that baby boy is fresh saskatoon berry pie!"

"I'll make you some!" hollered Lynnette, and she rushed over and grabbed up Little Andrew in her arms. "I'll make you a dozen pies right now."

When he heard that, Tub-o-Lard started smacking his big lips and his guts started making a noise like a D9 Cat walking on the roof. "That sounds good, Lynnette," he said. "Put some ice cream on it, will you."

"You stand right there, don't move!" And she ran into the house and closed the door. Lynnette was in a panic. The truth was she didn't know how to cook saskatoon berry pies. She didn't know how to cook anything.

"Oh, Lord! Oh, Lord!" she wailed. "Tub-o-Lard is going to eat up my brother for sure. If I could cook like Ma or Honey I could save him, but I can't."

"How are those pies coming?" called Tub-o-Lard from out in the yard.

"They're coming!" yelled Lynnette, and she started crashing pans around like she was cooking in a hurricane.

"All I can do is play the accordion!" she thought.

A minute or two later Lynnette walked out on the porch with a black leatherette box in her arms. Little Andrew followed along behind carrying a tin pot and a wooden spoon. "I thought you might like a little music while you waited for the pies to cook."

"That might be nice," said Tub-o-Lard.

Lynnette opened the box and took out her Harmonette Harmony Master accordion. She hung it off her shoulders, slipped her hands through the straps and started squeezing out the music.

She played "The Tennessee Waltz." Tub-o-Lard's big head started waving back and forth.

She played "Cripple Creek," and that big man started to skip a bit.

She played "Turkey in the Straw" and "The Beer Barrel Polka." Little Andrew was banging on the tin pan and laughing. Tub-o-Lard started to dance there in the middle of the yard. Lynnette played "The Silver Fox Polka." Little Andrew banged on the pot.

Tub-o-Lard was getting red in the face and the sweat was running down, but he couldn't stop dancing. "That was nice, Lynnette," he gasped. "You can stop now!"

But Lynnette didn't stop, and Little Andrew didn't stop either. They played "The Chock Full Polka" and "The Rambling Down Reel."

Tub-o-Lard danced and danced, and the sweat and the lard just poured off him. By the end of "The Athabaska Reel," he had shrunk down till he was no bigger than Walt Ferguson, and Walt Ferguson isn't all that big.

By the time Lynnette had finished playing "The Cockatoo Rag" and "Red Barn Afire," Tub-o-Lard had shrunk right out of his clothes and was dancing naked on the dry grass.

"Stop, Lynnette!" he pleaded. "I'm getting tired out."

"And hungry!" thought Lynnette, and she launched into "The Candy Candy Polka."

Tub-o-Lard shrunk down to the size of Little Andrew.

"No more," he called in a little baby voice.

"Just one more," said Lynnette, "The pies are almost ready!" She took a deep breath, and played "Rushin' By the Window" twice through without stopping.

That was the end of Tub-o-Lard. There was nothing left of that hungry man, but a pile of crumpled clothes and a great big greasy spot in the middle of the yard. Lynnette scooped up the clothes and stuffed them in the burning barrel.

She picked the baby up from the porch and gave him a big kiss. "Come on, Little Andrew," she said. "Let's go down to the Gateway Cafe and I'll buy you some saskatoon berry pie—with ice cream on the top."

THE GASTANK
OF MY HEART

O nce upon a time in the town of New Totem
near the western edge of the Vast Northern
Prairie there lived a boy named Eldrid. Eldrid
lived in a trailer up near Fish Creek with his two
mean and ugly brothers and his nasty, tick-in-
fested Pa.

His two brothers, Mean Albert and Ugly
Bill, loved to hunt, and they were forever stomp-
ing into the trailer with a dead moose or a bleed-
ing deer or some other kind of killed animal.
"Clean that thing, Eldrid!" Mean Albert would
snarl. Mean Albert was the talker; Ugly Bill just
whistled through the cracks in his teeth and
grinned a lot.

"We're going downtown, and we expect a pot
a stew when we get back. And don't forget to save
the tongue for Pa!" Eldrid's nasty Pa liked to eat

the tongues raw with just a little HP Sauce sprinkled on. So Eldrid would clean up the mess, skin out whatever unfortunate animal was on the menu that day and cook it up with some onions, carrots and potatoes. Eldrid would sing while he was working. He had a high, wailing voice, but there was a kind of magic about his singing. He didn't have a guitar, but he'd move his fingers like he was playing, and I swear, if you dropped a guitar into his hands, the music would come out perfect...

> The gastank of my heart is on the other side
>   of empty;
> My carburetor's all filled up with tears.
> The seat belt of my mind is hanging loose —
>   it's come unbuckled;
> And my oil pan is dragging, I do fear.
> OHHH, darling! OHHHH, darling!
> Your leaving me has really stripped my gears!

I'm not much of a singer, but you get the idea. Eldrid wrote that one himself, by the way.

Anyway, he was singing away, stirring the stew, when Mean and Ugly wheeled into the driveway in the pick-up truck.

Mean came running into the trailer whooping and hollering. "Where's Pa?" he hollered, "I got something I got to show him! Son of a gun! The old man's going to think he's got a porcupine in his pants, he'll be so tickled. Look at this, Eldrid!"

He was holding out a yellow piece of paper with a picture on it and some writing.

"What is it, Albert? Let me have a look."

"What's the magic word?" said Mean.

Eldrid sighed. "Please," he said.

"Please what?" Mean dangled the paper just out of Eldrid's reach.

"Please, sir," said Eldrid.

"What kind of please?"

"Pretty please, sir!"

"I didn't hear you..."

"Pretty, pretty please, sir!" said Eldrid. Mean gave him the paper. Sometimes the pleasing and sirring and prettying could go on most of the evening, but Mean was in a good mood that night. Eldrid looked at the paper. His heart stopped beating for the longest time, and, when it kicked in again, it started tearing along like a dog after the back tire of a pick-up truck.

"I don't believe this, Albert," he said, trying hard to keep his voice from shaking. "Cindy-Lou Pratt is coming here! She going to be coming here! Wow!"

"Give me that paper!" growled Mean, and he grabbed the paper out of Eldrid's hand.

"Wait! I mean...Please wait! I didn't see what day it is she's coming."

"What difference does it make?" said Mean. "You ain't going to see her. I don't want a lady like Cindy-Lou Pratt seeing you and me in the same room!" He slammed out the door and jumped in the pick-up.

The morning of the big day, Mean and Ugly and even Eldrid's nasty pa took baths, although, by the time that Pa got the water, he might as well not have bothered.

They sent Eldrid downtown to the laundromat with a couple garbage bags full of clothes to wash, and then set him to ironing everything for most of the afternoon. "I sure would like to see Cindy-Lou Pratt," Eldrid sighed as he flattened out the collar of Ugly's fanciest shirt – the one with pearl buttons and the peacock embroidered on the back.

"Don't be stupid, Eldrid," said Mean, "you can't go see no country and western singer. I mean – use your head! You don't have any pointy boots. You don't have a cowboy hat. You don't have a shirt with peacocks embroidered on it. What are you thinking about? And that reminds me – make sure you get a good shine on my pointy boots!"

So Eldrid stayed at home that night when Mean and Ugly and their nasty pa climbed into the pick-up and headed down to the high school to listen to Cindy-Lou Pratt and the Prattlers. Poor Eldrid was so sad, he thought he'd die. But instead of dying, he sat down on the porch step, and he tipped his head back, and he started to sing:

The headlights of my eyes are smeared with
 mud and bugs and dust now;
I cannot see to make it round the curves,
 dear.
The CB of your happy voice has ceased its
 sweet ten-four;
The crackle of the static's all I hear.
OHHH, darling! OHHH, darling!
Your leaving me has really stripped my gears!

I'm not much of a singer, but you get the idea.

I always said that there was something magic about that boy's singing, and what happened next just goes to prove the point.

A tall fellow, all dressed in gold–gold shirt, gold pants, gold cowboy hat, gold pointy boots, gold sunglasses–this gold fellow stepped around the corner and said, "Hi, how are you, kid?"

And Eldrid looked at this guy and said, "Who are you?"

The fellow smiled–he had gold teeth, too –he smiled and said, "Well, Eldrid, I'll tell you who I am. I'm your Fairy God Cowboy."

"Get out of here!" said Eldrid, and he got up and started to go in the trailer. He figured he had enough trouble with Mean, Ugly and nasty without having to put up with crazy, too.

"I thought you wanted to see Cindy-Lou," said the fellow, "I can fix it."

Eldrid stopped, "You know Cindy-Lou Pratt?"

"Let's just say I can fix it."

"Alright," said Eldrid "what do you want me to do."

"Just go over there and sit in that old Pontiac." There were half a dozen wrecked cars sitting around the trailer. The Pontiac that the golden fellow was talking about was sitting up on blocks with all four wheels gone. The engine was laying on the ground with grass growing up through the block.

Eldrid gave the guy a funny look, but he did what he was told.

"Grab hold of the wheel," said the golden fellow," and hang on tight." Eldrid grabbed the wheel, and as soon as he did, it was like he was going a thousand miles an hour. Things were whizzing by him in a blur. Eldrid just hung on—there was nothing else he could do. By and by, he stopped. He looked around and he was sitting in the parking lot at the high school. Guys in pointy boots and cowboy hats and girls in fancy dresses were walking by him, crowding up to the door.

"Well, are you going in or not?" Eldrid looked over and there was the gold cowboy sitting next to him.

"I can't go in there in a T-shirt and jeans . . ." Eldrid started to say. Then he looked down and he was wearing a blue satin shirt and shiny boots and a belt with a silver buckle on it and he looked good!

So Eldrid went in.

Well, Eldrid was starting to get a feel for how this was going now. He walked right up to the front. He just knew there'd be a seat sitting there empty—waiting for him. There was, too, and he sat down.

The lights went out. Bit by bit, the people got the idea, and pretty soon the only one in the whole gym still talking was Olive Rigley, and someone shushed her.

A fellow in a blue satin suit walked onto the stage, and set himself down behind the pile of drums. Another guy came on and picked up the bass guitar. One by one, the members of the band came out and took their places. They plinked and plunked a bit. They nodded at each other and adjusted their guitar straps, and all the while, the excitement was building in the gym.

Finally, the bass player bent down toward the mike and said: "Ladies and gentlemen! Cindy-Lou Pratt!"

To Eldrid the crash of clapping and hooting and whistling was like water sweeping down a gully. And then Cindy-Lou Pratt was there. She was singing, and she was singing just for him— lifting him, wringing him out, shaking him dry . . .

Then—SPLAT!—he was back in. The music had stopped and the crowd noise was flooding around.

If Eldrid hadn't been so lifted up he might have noticed how the amplifier cord had snaked out like a live thing and wrapped itself around the lead guitar player's feet just when the lead guitar player was heading into a bit of a pirou-ette. Well, now the lead guitar player was lying flat on his back not moving, the music was stopped and the crowd was growling.

Two of the other guys in the band lifted the lead guitar player up under the armpits and dragged him off the stage. And while they were doing that the golden man stepped in front of Eldrid and dropped a gold guitar right in his lap. He winked at Eldrid and walked through the door into the boy's locker room.

Cindy-Lou Pratt stepped up to the mike.

"Ladies and gentlemen," she said. The crowd got quiet. "Aaron fell and cracked his head pretty bad. I'm afraid..."

And then she looked right at Eldrid. She looked at him a long while. Eldrid could fell his ears starting to glow.

She said to him at last, "I just bet you know every one of my songs, don't you."

"Yes, ma'am," said Eldrid.

"Well, come on up here!" said Cindy-Lou. "We'll make sweet music together."

And that's exactly what they did.

When Mean Albert and Ugly Bill and their pa got out to the parking lot after the show, they saw that the pickup was wedged in between the side of the school and Cindy-Lou's bus, and some fool had dumped a wrecked '58 Pontiac right in back of it.

Mean and Ugly were grunting and puffing trying to shift the Pontiac when Cindy-Lou came out of the school. There was a skinny kid in a blue satin shirt with her, walking with his arm slipped through hers.

"Sing that last verse again," she said to the kid.

As they climbed on the bus Mean and Ugly could hear the kid singing:

> The spark plugs of my hopes have died since
>   we stopped sparking;
> My wipers cannot wipe away the tears.
> My trunk is full of sadness and the spare
>   now;
> And the honking of my horn gives me no
>   cheer.
> OHHHH, darling! OHHHH, darling!
> Your leaving me has really stripped my gears!

Mean put down his end of the Pontiac and jiggled his baby finger around in his ear.

"I heard that song before somewheres," he said. "I can't remember where I heard it though . . ."

"Who gives a damn!" snarled his pa. "Just move the car. I need a beer."

Right then the bus gave a toot, and backed out, and everybody was happy.

FUDGIE TROTTER'S BREAKAWAY

I don't know if they play so much now that they've got the new arena and regular teams with uniforms and everything, but when Fudgie Trotter was a boy, road hockey was a big thing. After the first couple of snowfalls, after the cars and trucks had had a chance to pack it down and slick it up, the kids would be out there on the icy roads with their hockey sticks and pucks, stick handling up and down the block.

Fudgie usually got to be the goalie, and that was okay with him. Fudgie didn't like to skate fast. Being goalie, he hardly ever had to skate fast.

Most road hockey games were a half a block long, a block at the most. But one winter, the game out in front of Fudgie's house started to stretch. Some kids from around the corner joined in, then some kids who lived up by the Esso

Station on the Airport Road. A whole family of boys who lived out by the grain elevators joined and then two kids who lived in a little cabin by the railway underpass on the highway. There were kids skating out of sideroads and poking the puck away, kids streaking down the hill into Tailor's Flats, flicking the puck across the bridge on the Peaceful River and passing to a teammate at the top of the hill on the other side. Before long the game stretched from in front of Fudgie Trotter's house in New Totem, across the Peaceful River, down the windy hill and across the Kiskatinaw River and up the hill on the other side, past the store at Farmington and right up to Eddie Fraser's house in Carson's Creek.

The game went on all through January that year, from early Saturday morning till late Sunday afternoon. Players came and players went, but Fudgie Trotter stood faithfully in his spot between two tin cans on the road in front of his house.

Fudgie's team was the stronger and the faster of the two, so Fudgie didn't see much action. Once, about the middle of January, a big kid with freckles got the puck and made a break for it. Fudgie saw him coming around the corner off 97th Street, and he braced himself for the shot. But Dale Swanson caught the freckle-faced kid before he could get his shot off, poked the puck away from him, turned and disappeared back up the road.

The game went on all through February. The same kid got a shot from the corner late on the afternoon of the 16th of February. Fudgie dived for it, but it dribbled past him and between the tin cans for a goal.

"Don't worry about it, Fudgie," Dale Swanson told him. "We're up forty-three to one anyway."

Then, on a Saturday afternoon in the middle of March, it happened. Fudgie was standing there in goal when the puck came wobbling up and stopped just a couple of yards from the goal. Fudgie waited for someone to come streaking around the corner, but nobody did.

Unbeknownst to Fudgie, there had been a big scuffle for the puck in front of the Lux Theatre in Tailor's Flats. About twenty kids from each team were poking away at the puck and jostling and shoving when someone noticed that there was a Roy Rogers movie playing at the theatre.

"This game has gone on too long," declared Dale Swanson. "Let's go to the show!"

The forty odd players roared their agreement. And with one final swipe at the puck, Dale called quits to the longest game of road hockey in the history of the Vast Northern Prairie.

That puck swished up the hill, around the corner by the underpass, along the Airport Road into town, down 97th Avenue and around the corner where it wobbled to a stop in front of Fudgie Trotter.

Fudgie was didn't know what to do. He knew he was supposed to stay there and guard the goal.

But there was the puck just laying there, and there was no one around. This was his chance – his first chance and maybe his only chance – for a breakaway.

Fudgie dashed forward, caught the puck on his stick and skated like he'd never skated before. He skidded around the corner and headed for the highway. He squinted up the road, expecting to see a rival player bulleting toward him. No one there.

"Schlick! Schlick! Schlick!" Fudgie's skates whispered rhythmically along the ice as he turned onto the highway and headed toward Carson's Creek.

"Click! Click! Click!" The puck tapped against his stick as he stick-handled it gracefully under the railway underpass.

"I wish Dale could see this!" he thought, but he knew that if Dale was there he'd be shouting, "Pass it, Fudgie! Give it to me! Pass it!" So he rocketed unseen down the hill and right on through Tailor's Flats. The momentum was enough to carry him across the bridge and most of the way up the other side.

Under the northern lights he skated on toward the Kiskatinaw River. He imagined crowds standing and cheering, stomping, whistling, the organ bleating, TAH TAH TAH. He imagined himself glancing up to grin in acknowledgement. But at that moment in his imagination the freckle-faced kid, taking advantage of Fudgie's split second of inattention, poked the puck away and went streaking back toward New Totem, where the goal stood empty and waiting.

Fudgie put his head down and swooped, uncheered but happy, across the bridge on the Kiskatinaw and on though the night.

He slicked and clicked past the store at Farmington in the silky grey light of dawn, and about noon the next day, skated into Carson's Creek, up 111th Avenue. Around the corner on Alaska Avenue, he stopped at the Royalite Station to ask if anyone knew where Eddie Fraser lived.

"As a matter of fact, Eddie's my boy," said the garage man. "I can take that puck to him for you if you like."

Fudgie was so tired that his knees were leaning on each other, but he took a deep breath and said, "No thank you, sir. I've got to do it myself." Eddie's father drew Fudgie a map, and off he skated. A few minutes later, he skated down Eddie's street. There were the two tin cans.

Fudgie got off his shot. It sailed straight as an arrow between the two tin cans, caroomed off a frozen lump of dirt and came to rest under a pick-up truck.

Fudgie threw his stick in the air, spun around twice, and skated off toward the bus station.

HIT THE ROAD RUNNING

Marvin Trotter got laid off from his job as driller with High Tower Oil early in the spring of the year that Andrew turned seven. To fill in till something else came up in the oil patch, he took a job helping with the haying at the Figget farm north of town.

Some days Marvin took Andrew and his little brother, Patrick, with him when he went to work and the two boys spent the day playing with the three Figget kids while Marvin and Gunther Figget were out in the field.

One evening, Marvin rounded up the two boys to head home, and while he was talking with Gunther for a few minutes about what needed to be done the next day, Andrew and Patrick climbed into the box of the old blue Ford pickup and waited. Marvin didn't mind them riding in the back if they didn't fool around.

Well, while they were waiting, Andrew noticed the tire iron laying in the box. The tire iron was the kind that's shaped like a silver cross with a socket at the end of each leg. And Andrew noticed a piece of rope there in back of the truck too. Don't ask me why it should have occurred to him that the rope and the tire iron should go together, but it did, and he tied the rope around the tire iron where the two pieces crossed. Andrew had never been a Boy Scout, but he figured he was pretty good at knots.

Marvin got done talking to Gunther Figget and came over to the truck. "If you two boys are going to ride in the back, I don't want any fooling around!" he said.

"We won't fool around!"

But as the blue Ford started bouncing down the Figget's long drive – it must have been a half mile – Andrew dropped the tire iron over the tailgate and fed out the rope until the tire iron was bouncing along the road.

It was real neat to watch! It skittered along bindity-bindity bing, and every time it hit a rock or a rut it would spin up into the air like it was alive – broing! You couldn't tell if it was going to leap to the left – pit-ting! – or jump to the right – bwang! And then it would skip along on its ends for a minute or so – bing! bing! bing! Neat!

Marvin must have glanced in the rear view mirror, though, because when they got to the main road, he stopped the truck and got and told the boys to haul the tire iron in and not be dragging it on the road anymore.

They started down the road heading south toward town.

"Andrew, what are you doing!" said Patrick.

Andrew had dropped the tire iron over the tailgate again, and was playing out the rope.

"Dad said we weren't supposed to drag it on the road. Well, I'm not going to drag it on the road. I'm just going to let it hang . . ."

And then the knot let loose, and the tire iron dropped onto the road, danced for a second – dwanga, dwanga, dwang – and lay there shining in the sun.

Andrew had to think fast. The old blue Ford was rattling along at close to twenty miles an hour and with every second the tire iron was getting further away and a darn good licking was getting closer.

This is how fast a thinker Andrew was. He thought all this: "I can jump out – we're not going that fast – I can jump out, I can run back and get the tire iron, and if I run as fast as I can across the pasture kitty corner, and Dad goes the regular way, I can probably get home just about the same time as him and he'll never even notice . . ." He thought all that and the tire iron was still only about fifty yards back.

He slid over the side of the box and stood on the running board, with his back to the ditch, and hung on to the edge of the box with both hands. Then he jumped.

For years afterwards, he wondered if he'd had time to think the problem through, and he'd jumped so that he hit the road running, if he'd have made it. But as it was, he flipped into the ditch and scraped along at just about twenty miles an hour for a quite a ways before he stopped up against a big rock.

He got up fast though.

As he crawled out of the ditch, he could hear his brother pounding on the window of the truck and yelling, "Andrew's dead! Andrew's dead!"

And it wasn't until Andrew was on his way back to pick up the tire iron that Marvin realized what Patrick was talking about and slammed on the brakes.

Normally, Marvin would have given Andrew a good licking right there in the road, but he was so happy to see that his boy was still alive that he forgot all about it.

It was a long time before Andrew forgave Patrick for squealing on him. But when he was a bit older he started figuring out fast a pick-up truck can go, even an old blue Ford, and how fast a boy can run across a hay meadow carrying a tire iron and the distances involved . . . And he had to admit to himself that he probably wouldn't have made it anyway—even if he'd hit the road running.

THE POPE'S CLUBHOUSE SANDWICH

The Pope never came to New Totem, and Meghan Spencer, for one, thanked God that he didn't.

Meghan was Dan and Gay Spencer's fourth child, the runt of the litter, red headed and freckled, with Coke bottle glasses and crossed eyes. She was six years old the year that the Pope didn't come to New Totem.

Dan was F.E. Spencer's youngest son, and the only one of five to take up the baker's trade. He was working the night shift at Spencer's Bakery in New Totem, the year that the Pope didn't come to town. F.E. worked the day shift, and Dan's brother Will and his wife, Dotty, took care of the customers out front and looked after all the ordering for the grocery store, the hotel and the two cafes.

Most Saturdays, Dan's kids were down at the bakery. Meghan's older sister, Sally, helped out behind the counter serving doughnuts and coffee. She got to wear a uniform, and she even got paid a bit. F.E. usually found some work for Normie and Doug to do in the back – moving sacks of flour around, sweeping the floor, or running the bread slicing machine.

Meghan was kind of little to be of much use, but she loved to hang around just the same. You'd think that the thing that a kid would like about having the run of a bakery would be the sweet stuff – the cookies and the cakes and the doughnuts – but Meghan didn't care all that much for sweet food. What she loved about the bakery was the smell of baking bread. She loved all the shining stainless steel, and the big mixer with the dough hook flinging the bread dough around – womp! womp! womp! She loved the warmth of the ovens, and the ghost dusting of flour on the table tops. She loved to stand at the counter and listen to the grown-ups talking, to hear the bell over the door ring when anybody went in or out, and the chang of the cash register.

And she loved the feel of the dough. Most times, F.E. would give her a big hunk of bread dough to knead and shape. She loved the smoothness of it, and the way it bounced back under her fingers like there was a life in there swelling to get out.

"Wash your hands," F.E.'d say. He was a stickler for cleanliness. But no matter how hard she washed, her dough ended up a kind of pasty grey colour by the time she had it ready for the pan. And it always came out of the oven with a crust about a half an inch thick which suited Meghan just fine, because the crust was what she liked best.

That Saturday, F.E. noticed right away the band-aid on Meghan's finger, and he asked her did she get a cut. Meghan told him, "Yes, Grandpa. I was helping Mom peel the carrots, and I peeled off the end of my finger." Tears came into her eyes just at the thought of it.

"It hurts," she said.

"I don't imagine you'll be wanting to make bread today with your finger hurting like that," F.E. said. He was just in the process of tipping a batch of bread out of the mixer bowl onto the table where he'd knead it and portion it out into loaves.

Meghan shook her head, no.

"Well, you wait right here," he said. "I'll get you a doughnut from out front." Even though Meghan didn't care for doughnuts, she'd never told F.E. – nor anyone else, for that matter. Somehow, it seemed to her that if all those people kept wanting to give her doughnuts, she SHOULD like them. Even if she didn't.

So F.E. wiped his hands on his apron where it stretched across his belly, and went to get Meghan her doughnut. Meghan stood there thinking how it was too bad that she wasn't going to get to make some bread, and wondering if her finger really hurt all that much. Maybe it was healed up enough that she could manage. She put her hand on the big mound of dough on the table and gave it a push; it didn't bother her finger at all. Then she pointed her finger and pushed it all the way into the dough right as far as it would go.

"That doesn't hurt much," she thought. "I'm going to tell Grandpa that I want to make some bread."

Right then F.E. came back. Meghan snatched her hand back. F.E. would give her heck for touching the dough without washing her hands. He was a stickler for cleanliness.

"Here's your doughnut, Meg!" said F.E.

Meghan reached for the doughnut.

"You took off your band-aid?" said F.E.

Meghan glanced at her finger. The band-aid was gone.

"Is your finger better then?"

"Yes, Grandpa," whispered Meghan.

"So do you want to make some bread?"

He picked up a scraper and began to cut the mound of dough into two smaller mounds. Meghan watched round-eyed and quaking with dread. What would her grandpa say when he found the band-aid?

"Not going to bake bread today, eh?" said her grandfather. "Why don't you go out and sit at the counter and eat your doughnut then.

"Okay, Grandpa," whispered Meghan.

She sat at the counter with her doughnut sitting in front of her like a sugary rebuke. She was waiting for her grandfather to come out and start yelling at her. As soon as he found that band-aid he was going to come out yelling. He was a stickler for cleanliness. He would probably never let her come into the bakery again.

Her grandfather came out from the back. He didn't yell, though. He poured himself a cup of coffee.

"Are you finished the bread making, Grampa?" asked Meghan.

"It's in the proofer," said F.E. "I'll put it in the oven before I go home and your dad can take it out when he comes to work."

"Thank you, God!" Meghan prayed silently to herself. "He didn't find it!" She ate her doughnut in four bites, determined to enjoy it, to show her gratitude for being spared.

"Think about it, Noodle," Normie said to her on the way home. "If Grandpa didn't find the band-aid, where is it?"

"I don't know," said Meghan.

"I'll tell you," said Normie.

"I shouldn't tell Normie my secrets," Meghan reminded herself. But it was too late this time.

"Your band-aid is in somebody's loaf of bread! That's where it is."

"Yuck!" said Doug. "Was there blood on it? Yuck!"

"And when someone finds that band-aid . . ." Normie rolled his eyes dramatically. "You think you had trouble before!"

"I heard about a woman who found a fly in a bottle of Coke," chimed in Doug. "And she sued the Coca Cola Company for a million dollars, and they had to pay!"

"Grandpa doesn't have a million dollars," said Normie. "I guess he'd have to sell the bakery."

"What if somebody important finds it—someone like the mayor!" said Doug.

"He'll take away grandpa's license and close the bakery," said Normie.

"Dad'll be out of a job," said Doug.

Meghan started to cry.

"Hey! There's no use crying about it!" said Normie. "There's nothing you can do now but wait and hope nobody actually eats the thing!"

Meghan waited. All afternoon, all through supper, bathtime and storytime, she waited. Any minute her father was going to come shuffling in with his head hanging down, and he'd say, "The bakery's closed down, Gay. The kids are going to starve. We'll have to send them to Edmonton to live with Margaret."

But by bedtime, he still hadn't arrived home.

As she was going up to bed, Meghan asked her mom, "Mom, who is the most important person in the world?"

"I suppose it would have to be the Pope," said her Mom. "But you're important to me."

Meghan couldn't sleep. She lay in the dark listening to her sister's quiet breathing.

It wasn't likely, but it could happen! Say the Pope come did come to town? He would go to the

Thunderbird Hotel for lunch, wouldn't he! And he'd sit in the booth right by the window where Hal Parker, the barber, and all his friends always sit. But they'd have to move because the Pope was more important. They wouldn't mind moving for the Pope. And the Pope would order a clubhouse sandwich, because he was rich. And when the clubhouse sandwich came, the Pope would lift up the pickle from the top and put it on the side of the plate. And then he'd look down and he'd see the band-aid stuck right into the top piece of bread. He'd be mad. He'd say, "Who baked this bread! I'm a stickler for cleanliness, and I won't stand for band-aids in my bread! I want to know who baked this bread!" And when they told him, "F.E. Spencer," he'd go stomping across the street, his robes flying out behind him like a kite. And he would go into the bakery, right into the back where customers weren't allowed to go and he'd. . . he'd excommunicate her grandpa! (Meghan wasn't sure how he'd do that, but she knew F.E. wouldn't like it!)

But, no! God wouldn't let the Pope do that, because it wasn't F.E.'s fault. There would be a miracle! God would appear in the bakery looking like a giant gingerbread man, and He would say, "Meghan did it. It wasn't F.E.'s fault! I saw Meghan stick her finger into the dough, and she didn't even wash her hands first!"

Meghan started to whimper. She slid out from under the covers and crawled over to Sally's bed. She shook her sister until Sally opened one bleary eye. "What is it, Meggie? What's the matter?"

"You have to help me, Sally," Meghan sobbed. "I'm going to Hell! I'm going to Hell!"

Well, finally Sally got her calmed down, and Meghan told her the whole story.

"It's okay, Meggie," Sally said, stroking her hair back from her face. "The Pope is in Rome, and the Vatican announced today that he's got no plans at all to visit New Totem."

"Are you sure?" said Meghan.

"I'm sure," said Sally.

And then Meghan went to sleep.

The next morning at breakfast, Normie started to choke on something when he was eating his toast. Everybody took turns whacking him on the back, except Meghan who was edging toward the door. But Normie kept going, "Kaaa . . . kaaa . . . kaaa!" And then he jumped up and ran to the bathroom.

Everybody sat there looking at everybody else for a part of a minute, and then Dan got up to see if Normie was alright. But before he could get to the bathroom, Normie came back out. He was really pale, but otherwise he seemed okay.

"Something go down the wrong tube, son?" said Dan.

Normie looked over at Meghan, and then he grinned, and he said, "Yeah, I guess."

Meghan was glad. It's a nice feeling, knowing you've been saved from going to Hell.

DRIFTED IN

Just off the Clayhurst Road, north of New Totem, you can see a solitary pine tree standing out above a clump of smaller pines. And if you look twice, you'll notice that the top ten, twelve, feet of that tree are missing–lopped off clean. Most people just assume it was lightning or the wind that took off the top of that tree, but I'll tell you the real story.

Arnie Dewhurst nodded off while drinking cocoa out of a thermos in the cab of his pick-up truck. He dreamed about how, in a couple of hours, he would top up Ethel and head back to town to spend Christmas Eve with his lovely wife, Honey, and his darling daughter, Brandy.

But when he woke up the windshield was a blank white sheet. The pick-up truck was en- cased in white–back, front and sides.

Sometimes, on the Vast Northern Prairie, the wind comes whining and yammering out of the west, raking every crumb of loose snow before it. It takes that snow and shoves it with its icy fingers into every crack and crevice, stomps on it with its frozen feet, packing it down, until the land, and everything in it, is locked in tight. It can happen without any warning at all. One minute, you're sitting in your pick-up truck sipping cocoa and dreaming about Christmas at home and, the next minute, you're drifted in!

"Drifted in!" grumbled Arnie.

He reached under the seat for the short handled shovel that is carried at all times in every pick-up truck on the Vast Northern Prairie for just such emergencies.

He started to dig. He dug out and up, heading for the top of the drift. He knew better than to dig straight out, hoping to find the Cat. A friend of his had tried that. He'd missed the front of the Cat by a couple of feet and had kept on burrowing away for a month or more before a Chinook came along and melted all the snow. He'd found himself on his hands and knees in front of Rexall's Drug Store in Pine Bluff looking like a fool.

Several hours later, Arnie's head poked up above the top of the snow. The wind had died down, and the late afternoon sky was a pearly pink. A hundred yards to the east a thin plume of smoke rose out of a wide crater in the snow. Arnie pulled himself out of the hole and scampered over to the edge of the crater. There, forty feet below, was Ethel, Arnie's big yellow D9 Caterpillar Crawler Tractor, purring contentedly.

Arnie scrambled down the side of the crater and up into the driver's seat. He took a minute to let Ethel's heat soak into his bones – it was the heat of the great engine that had prevented the snow from burying Ethel in the first place, of course – then he engaged the clutch and started to dig his way out.

Arnie crawled the Cat up to the top of the drift. Ethel was no lightweight, but the snow was packed in tight, and she walked along on top with no problem at all.

Arnie pointed her blade south-west toward the town of New Totem and settled back to enjoy the scenery. Cutting across country he'd be home in time to tuck Brandy into bed. He was happy.

The moon poked its fat pink nose out of the snow and started to climb the wide arc of the sky. The great flat desert of snow glistened and shimmered. Suddenly, Arnie saw a dark shape against the whiteness – a man waving his arms and jumping up and down.

"Well, I'll be a bucktoothed beaver if that isn't Orville Potts!"

Orville Potts was a grader operator working out of the Bolger Bros. camp at Badger Bog.

"I must have come farther than I figured," thought Arnie.

"Hallo, there, Orville. What's up?"

Orville Potts climbed up onto Ethel, and he and Arnie yelled back and forth at each other.

"The camp's drifted in, Arnie!"

"I got drifted in myself! How come you don't dig yourself out?"

"New kid started this week, he shut down all the machines when we came in for lunch. We couldn't get them started again before the wind came up."

Arnie shook his head gravely. The fourth Rule of Survival on the Vast Northern Prairie—or maybe it's the third—states: You never shut your machine down from the middle of October to the middle of May, because you might never get it started again.

"Well, if you're going to get home for Christmas, I guess I'll have to dig you out!" yelled Arnie.

He lowered Ethel's blade and started digging.

The moon was riding high in the sky when he pushed the last of the snow away from the cook shack door.

"Thanks for digging us out, Arnie," said Cook, handing Arnie a steaming mug of tea, "now we just got to figure some way of getting to town."

"Never thought about that," said Arnie. He slurped his tea and thought about it.

"Soon as I get Ethel fuelled up," he said as he drained his mug, "we'll hook the cook shack on behind, and I'll give you a tow to town."

That's what they did, and, within the hour, they were skidding along over the snow toward New Totem. Arnie and Orville rode up front on Ethel and the rest of the men sat around the table in the cook shack eating butter tarts, drinking tea and singing Christmas carols.

"It might be a bit tricky crossing the Beaten River," Orville yelled to Arnie.

Between them and town, the Beaten River flowed through a deep gorge. A snakey road wound down one side of the gorge and up the other, but finding the road was going to be no easy matter.

"We'll have to cross that river when we come to it," yelled Arnie.

A ways further along Orville yelled, "Stop the Cat a minute, Arn. I'm going to cut us a Christmas tree."

He grabbed up Arnie's power saw and headed off across the drift toward a scrag of a pine tree that was sticking out of the snow. In a few minutes he was back, dragging the tree behind him.

"Hey, Cook!" he called. "Got any Christmas lights stashed in there?"

"I believe I might!" Cook hollered back.

The men hoisted the tree to the top of the cook shack, and, while Ethel chugged along over the snow, they strung lights on it and decorated it with tin-foil stars and popcorn strings.

Just as they were putting one last star right on the top of the tree, Newel Trivet spotted a light on the horizon.

"It's the Rig!" shouted Harve Westaway jumping up and down like a crazy man on top of the cook shack. "It's the Rig! The Rig!"

Unless you've been to New Totem, you might be wondering what Harve was so excited about. On the highest bit of ground in New Totem—which isn't a lot higher than the lowest bit—right in front of the curling rink, a few years ago, they put up a huge oil derrick. It was put there to honour all the oil workers of the Vast Northern Prairie—"Past, present and future. . ." as the Mayor said on the occasion. And that is what Harve Westaway saw, all covered, as it is every year, with blinking, twinkling Christmas lights.

"We'll be home for Christmas!" yelled Harve.

The men sent up a cheer that echoed off the moon, although it wasn't until the night of the twenty-seventh of December that it finally came back. Mrs. Tailor down on the Tailor's Flats heard the echo and thought it was a wolf. But old Gus Tailor said to her, "Go back to sleep, Flo. It's just those boys from up at Badger Bog, happy to be home for Christmas."

And none was happier than Arnie Dewhurst, when he drove Ethel up beside the trailer out on Longman Road and saw Honey and Brandy standing there on the porch waving to him.

Brandy squirmed out of her mother's arms and clambered up to onto Ethel and gave her father a great big smoochy Christmas kiss.

"Merry Christmas, Daddy!" she yelled.

That night a Chinook blew in, and by Boxing Day most of the snow was gone.

You're probably wondering why I never said anything about how Arnie and his friends got across the Beaten River that Christmas Eve.

It's only supposing, of course, but since there is no way to get to New Totem from Badger Bog without crossing the Beaten, and since no one remembers crossing it, Arnie Dewhurst supposes that the gorge was drifted in solid, and they rode right over it without even noticing it was there.

I started off to tell you about the missing top of that pine tree, didn't I? Well, that was Orville Potts' Christmas tree, of course.